"Mary continues in all of her books to understand Truth comes from the Bible. God gives to us the necessary Truth to handle all problems in our lives. Her books reflect this understanding of life."

Gordon Hendrickson, Acts 6 Missions

"Mary is a rising star in the Lord's galaxy of Biblically sound
writers."

Suzanne Geiss...Founder of Woofi the Missionary Puppy
Ministry

Back to the Beginning...

◆

Remembering Your First Love

Mary Barrett

iUniverse, Inc.
New York   Bloomington

Back to the Beginning...
Remembering Your First Love

iUniverse books may be ordered through booksellers or by contacting:

*iUniverse
1663 Liberty Drive
Bloomington, IN 47403
www.iuniverse.com
1-800-Authors (1-800-288-4677)*

*Because of the dynamic nature of the Internet, any Web addresses or
links contained in this book may have changed since publication and may
no longer be valid. The views expressed in this work are solely those of
the author and do not necessarily reflect the views of the publisher, and
the publisher hereby disclaims any responsibility for them.*

ISBN: 978-1-4401-3369-5 (pbk)
ISBN: 978-1-4401-3370-1 (ebk)

Printed in the United States of America

iUniverse rev. date: 8/4/2009

Little Ewe

There was a little sheep that knew what she had to do
The Shepherd told her, "Walk over here, little ewe"
She looked at the way she should go
But it was too far and she said, "No"
She disobeyed and sat in the dirt
The Shepherd sat Beside His little ewe
And said "This is what you have to do"
I will go with you, so you're not alone
With My strength and your little legs
You soon will be home
Time on earth is very brief
And you're spending too much time with a thief
I have great blessings and joy that abound
So please little sheep, get off the ground
Rita Barrett 1/27/05

Dedication and Thanks

This writing is dedicated to the continued glory of God. I am filled with such a grateful heart for all the support of those who are walking beside me, especially my sisters in life and my sisters in Christ.

Table of Contents

Invitation

Hosea 2: 14-15 (NLT*) – "But then I will win her back once again. I will lead her out into the desert and speak tenderly to her there. I will return her vineyards to her and transform the Valley of Trouble into a gateway of hope. She will give herself to me there, as she did long ago when she was young, when I freed her from her captivity in Egypt."

Come study the love God has for His people. He remembers the day our relationship began, but do we? That relationship has been there from the beginning, and He is waiting for us to go back again. By embarking on a spiritual journey, we have the opportunity to experience a personal love story. Each story introduces us to what we have to gain and to forget, through which we can return to the greatest love ever known. By remembering God's great love, we can begin to turn back from the furthest point. Just when it feels like it's time to give up, the heart longs to be reconnected with the love that was shared at the beginning, and so we go back to meet again.

We all want our name to be whispered by someone who will be faithful to us. Here we will reflect on and consider for ourselves the total essence of wondrous love. Our name is known by a King who desires to take our troubles away; He is waiting to walk through the gateway of hope with you. Isn't that exciting? Most of us want to attain a life of purpose, passion, and productivity. A life without a heart-to-heart connection with the Spirit of God is a life without the spark of a bright fire burning alive in our soul.

This invitation is for anyone who has or is seeking to embark on a path headed to God. There never is and never will be a time when we stop needing God. As we embark on our journey through the following pages, allow yourself to be drawn into the stories both from the Bible and from everyday life experience. Embracing how much love our Heavenly Father has for us and how faithful He remains to our relationship even when we forget, we will realize this message of hope. Through scripture we will be captivated and swept away by God's love letter to us. This letter says, "If we are unfaithful, He remains faithful, for He cannot deny Himself" (2 Timothy 2:13). God will be there on our side, even in the midst of so much turmoil that causes us to doubt whether there is any spiritual connection left.

Take a moment each day to sit back, devoting special time to reflect upon the day you will personally meet the eternal lover of our soul. If you have yet to make a heart-to-heart connection, now is always the perfect time to consider letting that love into your life. The awesome gift we are given, once connected, is that we will have a beginning that has no end! Faithfulness is the trusted place in which God holds our hearts, melting our fears until we remember it is He to whom we desire to return. Let's begin our journey with these words as our starting point: "…For I know the One whom I have trusted, and I am sure that He is able to guard what I have entrusted to Him until the day He returns." Let's prepare ourselves to re-write a love story with God that always ends with a "happily ever after."

* The New Living Translation (NLT) version of the Bible is referenced throughout the book.

Introduction

Why do we find ourselves returning to the beginning of our relationship with God and reconnecting our hearts to His? As I study God's Word, I have developed a deeper understanding about His people and our tendency to become unfaithful to the word of God. The long, distinguished list of those who have met with fallen human nature is woven all through the Bible. Good people get knocked off course at times, letting their connection with God weaken. Ultimately, these souls make the choice to return back to the beginning of their relationship to reconnect and do the right thing. Some of these names may be familiar ones; Moses, Jonah, Abraham, Jacob, and Joseph are all counted among those whose stories of recommitment to faithfulness to God provide us an example. When we lose sight of that intimate connection with our Creator, it is up to us to look back and remember the commitment God has made to us, His people. "I will be faithful to you and make you mine, and you will finally know me as Lord" (Hosea 2:20).

The study we shared in <u>Hanging on the Vine</u> in the first book of the *Mother in Love Series* illustrates our need to establish God's Word in our lives to form a foundation of love, joy, peace, patience, kindness, goodness, gentleness, and self-control. The fruit of the Holy Spirit is our trusted source to turn to when life presents trials beyond what we can cope with. Every tool we need for eternal life is connected to the faithfulness of God and our belief in His Son Jesus. The Father, Son, and Holy Spirit communicate with us where it matters: at the heart.

As with any relationship we value, our relationship with God must be nurtured. In this, the second devotional study, we will examine circumstances that cause us to take our eyes off our spiritual relationship with the Lord. This is the lesson we must incorporate into our spiritual journey if we are to endure the trials we will encounter. Every circumstance depends on the solidity of the initial spiritual connection when it was established. We now know that the connection we make with God provides all the seeds that will produce the fruit our lives aspire to produce. The challenge we face now is keeping that connection vibrant so that the spark of our spiritual life does not burn out!

All of us start at the same place on our journey in connecting to God, at the throne of grace, which is the gift of love and mercy given to us so that we can complete our race on earth with victory. We maintain a greater knowledge of what we want our connection to be if we cling to these words: "And let us run with endurance the race that God has set before us. We do this by keeping our eyes on Jesus, on whom our faith depends from start to finish" (Hebrews 12:1-2).

The place from which we all must start is also our ultimate ending place – with God. This study provides a way to connect back to a faithful friend who is waiting for us to remember all that is good about being together. These stories will offer encouragement as they communicate how faithful God is to us. Since the Bible tells us that we are in the image of the Creator, all of our stories have begun at the same place: in the heart of God.

Let's now begin with open minds and a grateful prayer. Mediate on these words as you consider making them your own. "You saw me before I was born. Every day of my life was recorded in your book. Every moment was laid out before a single day had passed. How precious are your thoughts about me, O God! They are innumerable! I can't even count them; they outnumber the grains of sand! And when I wake up in the morning you are still with me!" (Psalm 139:16-18).

Roadside Conversion

There are times when one needs to seize an opportunity, striking while the iron is hot. My connection with God and Jesus was established just that way, in an instant. Certain moments we experience can leave behind impressions that make every element about it feel as fresh as the day it happened. My senses still recall each detail of this scene leading to the beginning of what would become a beautiful relationship.

During the sweltering month of July 1994, I was at a strange point in my 24-year-old life. I was new to motherhood, still young in my marriage, and very unsure yet if I was doing anything right. During those early, awkward years of discovery, my husband's mother lovingly took me under her wing. She slowly began telling me the story of her relationship with God and His Son – a relationship I had yet to encounter. There was something wonderful about the way she lived her life, and it made others want everything she had. As I observed her life and listened to her story of Jesus, she prayed that my heart would be motivated, and my eyes clearly opened to what eternity offered.

I adored my mother-in-law, so when she asked me to help the Bible study class in serving dinner at a woman's gathering, I agreed. We had an incredible time fellowshipping with these women. Leaving with uplifted spirits, aching feet, and the lingering smell of homemade iced tea and pound cake, she and I had plenty to talk about on the way home. Neither one of us knew that the car ride home would spark our desire for a complete heart connection to God. Every time I smell pound cake, I am mentally transported back and filled with immeasurable gratitude to the woman who told me what she felt she needed to share.

This story demonstrates the strength of two people who listened to each other, allowing God to enter in. Scripture clearly says, "For where two or three gather together because they are mine, I am there among them" (Matthew 18: 20). My mother-in-law heard the things that I wanted in my life, and she pointed out the only way I could get them. I was ready to accept the invitation to connect with a Christ-centered life.

There was no time wasted; how this dear lady could move when the Holy Spirit was moving her! Three blocks before we reached my driveway, she zipped into an alley, and, parking next to a dumpster asked me if I wanted to trade my earthly "trash" for eternal "treasure" forever. My answer, as you could guess, was yes, and Jesus went from the back seat to the driver's seat of my life that hot summer night. That was the true beginning to my walk with the Lord.

Of course, this does not mean that maintaining my relationship with God has been easy. Over the years I have done my share to garble the line of communication, causing much unpleasant static in my life! But never did God leave me, and never did I fail to find Him there when I needed to bring my heart back to His!

Be blessed as you read stories of those who decided to go back to God and keep the connection alive.

Format of Devotions

At the end of each chapter will be a section called Questions To Begin With. These questions provide opportunities and ideas to start to make a connection with God using your personal experiences. The act of reflecting on these questions serves to help you better understand where your spiritual relationship is and if you are comfortable with where that relationship is.

After the Questions To Begin With section, please use the suggested scripture readings as a guide for your time to connect with God's Word. The Bible references pertain to the "connection" you read about in the devotion story. As you spend time delving into the Scriptures to Connect to section, your desire will deepen to be heart-to-heart with God.

My favorite practice in reflective study is recording all of the personal moments that have been revealed to me. This is why plenty of blanks pages have been provided on which you can record your personal thoughts! Each chapter has a special space in which you can include your questions and impressions. At the back of the book are pages entitled "I am Going Back To…?" that encourage you to record prayers of your own along with any other moments of contact with God you have been given during your journey in connecting yourself to a spiritual journey.

Chapter One: Making the Connection

A Connection to God's Heart – "Draw close to God and God will draw close to you." -James 4:8

What a beautifully simple verse to present how our connection to God can be realized. Making initial contact with God requires us to take our focus off this world and turn our attention to being with Him. God is close to those who want to be close to Him. The point of our efforts is to make things of the spirit what we desire to draw near to. We are not left to guess how to accomplish this closeness so that we can feel and know the presence of God in our lives. The word of God is the connection from our heart to His. Our journey in our spiritual relationship grows as we open our minds to the wisdom that is revealed, leading us to use it in our lives as much as we can. Taking time daily to read God's Word keeps us inspired to walk closer and strengthen our connection.

Further expounding upon the idea of wisdom being revealed to us, I was taught an interesting new word: polarity. Polarity is defined in the dictionary as an attraction toward a particular object or a pull in a specific direction. What an effective way to describe the vision of what a spiritual connection is! The polarity of God is what draws us closer to the specific destination we want to reach, His heart. So, it would seem that a journey towards heaven is one pulling us towards God! God's polarity is the magnetic force that never breaks the connection it makes and is big enough to carry the weight of any person who wants to apply him- or herself to it. The closeness of God is vast enough for all of us to be part of it.

Now that we are gaining a clearer understanding of the attraction towards God, we can begin the process of getting connected. Let's look at what an actual connection is made of. What do we need to be willing to do in our attempt to make a real spark occur in our lives? For me, it was delving deeper into God's Word and pursuing God. This turned out to be a crucial element for me, because the more I learned, the more I wanted to know. We cannot become intimate in any relationship before we know the person we are interested in.

The Bible is ours to open as the gateway to eternity. Not only does the Bible invite us in, but we are also quickly exposed to the message that we are valued and wanted by our Creator. Psalm 139 erases any doubt about our origin or purpose by which we were designed. I encourage reading in its entirety this poem of creativity, but for the moment, verses 13 and 14 highlight the above point. "You made all the delicate, inner parts of my body and knit me together in my mother's womb. Thank you for making me so wonderfully complex!

Your workmanship is marvelous…" Reading this excerpt, do you want to know more? As we involve ourselves and explore each verse from this Psalm, what becomes unmistakable is that we were made to be with God. When we are separated or disconnected, we experienced an unmistakable void in our hearts. Because we are loved by our Heavenly Father so completely, He waits to be let in. This incredible gift of being in close contact with the spiritual world emphasizes that everyone can know spiritual truth, sound doctrine, and scriptural facts for the purpose of generating an intimate personal friendship with Christ, leading to a transformed way of living. You can experience for yourself what happens when we trust God by letting him into our lives. "May the Lord bring you into an ever deeper understanding of the love of God…" (2 Thessalonians 3:5). The invitation to re-establish that connection will always be there, although never demanded, while we are here on earth. The freedom to walk toward wherever we want to be forever remains yours and mine.

The promises of God are anchored in His unchanging character. Sometimes even our most heartfelt promises will falter, but the Word of God is filled with the steadfast promise that His love never fails! The promises given to us are never taken away because of our earthy actions of good and bad behavior. Just because we are good, God does not love us more, and neither does He leave us when we stumble in moments of poor choices and rebellion. God seizes those opportunities to be gracious to His people – yes, that includes you and me.

In the Gospel of Matthew, we discover Jesus teaching a multitude of people on a mountainside in Galilee. The ministry of Jesus was spreading the Good News about the Kingdom of Heaven. Many people wanted the answer to the question of how the connection to God is made. He taught them, "God blesses those who realize their need for Him for the Kingdom of Heaven is given to them" (Matthew 5:3). Jesus told the crowd that human nature does not want to connect with what there is no need for. Once we figure out that God's presence in our lives in a basic need, the spiritual quest to connect with the source that will fill it in begins.

Being persistent in making a clear connection to heaven begins with our commitment to tuning into God and tuning out the noisy, dark distractions that surround us. Once the switch goes on, the bright Light of the World invades the dimmest regions of our wondering hearts!

QUESTIONS TO BEGIN WITH

- Do you personally want to draw nearer to God? What does that type of closeness mean to you?

- How close is God to you right now?

- Is the depth of spiritual connection you want present in your life yet?

- After making the initial connection to God, what are some things that will help keep it alive?

- From what has been shared in this chapter, what does God offer as His connection to us?

- Read Psalm 139 and write what God reveals specially to you.

SCRIPTURES TO CONNECT TO

Hebrews 8:10, 1 Corinthians 1:9, Psalm 1:1 & 107:9, Exodus 33:14

Matthew 5:8, Genesis 28:15, Isaiah 25:9, 2 Corinthians 5:17

Personal Moments

Personal Moments

Chapter Two: Back to the Call of a Heart

A Connection to God's Heart – "And so, my children listen to me, for happy are all who follow my ways. Listen to my counsel and be wise. Don't ignore it. Happy are those who listen to me, watching for me daily at my gates, waiting for me outside my home! For whoever finds me finds life and wins approval from the Lord." -Proverbs 8: 32-35

Happiness is the essential ingredient vital to sustaining a fulfilled existence. The emotion of happiness is indeed something temporarily dictated by external events, but happiness in your spiritual walk with the Lord can be trusted and lasting, because although the world changes with each new whim, God remains consistent. God wants to speak to us. He whispers His truths into the corners of our hearts, allowing them to linger there until we are ready to hear them. Once our hearts soften and the veil between us and God is taken down, we begin to explore who He is. If we are open to what we are exposed to, we encounter happiness from a place many will not accept. God calls each one of us to be part of His family, but we need to hear it first.

Those who are alert and respond to the Spirit's voice are given eternity.

The call comes from deep inside us, and although it is sometimes hard to identify, "Let those who are wise understand these things. Let those who are discerning listen carefully. The paths of the Lord are true and right, and righteous people live by walking in them" (Hosea 14:9). This word of Scripture tells us that our knowledge comes when we submit our thoughts to God as the source of all wisdom. I believe before we can know what we are feeling, we need to hand our understanding to God. Doing that will always ensure the correct outcome!

Did you know that it is quite possible to be in two places at one time? This came as a surprise to me, but the explanation I was given broadened my understanding. The moment a heart hears and connects with that call to Jesus, we begin living out the purpose of heaven while still here on earth. The carnal nature, which is our flesh, merges with our spiritual nature, which is the spirit within us. We live in both worlds, having a spiritual nature in our relationship with God the Father and Jesus the Son. Our earthy journey takes place where we live in the flesh, and our spiritual relationship exists where we live with God each day. Of course, not everyone will experience both worlds; many settle for what they see and refuse to enter into that which they have not yet faith to accept.

Those who have learned how to develop inner joy are those who have yielded to the call of what God purposed their life to be. Listening and learning from God is what equips us to know how to live when we are bombarded with innumerable and indiscernible voices.

So, the question we hope to answer is this: How do I know what God is calling me to do with my life? In order to discover the answer, I suggest actively asking, listening, waiting, and then acting on what God communicates to you. An authentic heart will always get an answer. "If you listen to God's word and apply it, you will receive a blessing" (Luke 11:28).

Some of us are blessed because we step up to the call that God has placed in our hearts. He offers this same connection to anyone; God has no favorite children. In this, an ordinary life becomes exceptional. Have you ever met anyone with so much energy from the Holy Spirit that it just shines contagiously from every part of them? Surely a person like that has experienced something powerful, causing others to want to experience it too! I know several people who, after falling deeply in love with the awesome spirit of Jesus, experienced a change of heart that was undeniable.

Some have shared with me that the promptings the "still, small voice" told them they possessed a gift that needed to be shared and exercised. God will use people around us to make us aware of what we do not see for ourselves. In this manner, John's story began.

John's story:

A very gifted and special young man, John was unaware of a lady who had been watching him and his wife sitting in the pews of their snug, little suburban church. One particular Sunday, the pastor issued a plea that people were needed to work with the youth. As this young couple prepared to leave the service, this lady confronted them and clearly had a message she wanted to convey. She told John that the joy on his face she saw each week provided evidence enough for her that he loves the Lord and that God wants to use him. With complete conviction, she concluded the conversation by saying, "You are what the youth need; now you need to go home and pray about this."

John, who was shy by nature, smiled and offered no real verbal reply as he and his wife left. He was challenged to answer a call that he had no idea was even there! He and his wife decided they would indeed pray about it and concluded that they would become the youth group leaders. John and Jen began a powerful ministry to the youth that has impacted more lives than we can count. This couple started their efforts with seven youth in the basement of a cottage church. John's passion and talent for singing, songwriting, drawing, and most of all preaching the Gospel to the youth led him down a road that he could not have imagined in his wildest dreams. The couple are now serving more then 300 youth weekly and ministering to their needs in a place much further from where they started. But the trip to the desired destination did contain detours. John and his small family first packed their bags and headed to the state of Georgia, but God had other plans for them. They encountered problems with selling their home and other details that brought them back to our small church, whose members excitedly welcomed them back. This celebration for the congregation was short lived, because God did call John to where he was to go. Packing again to say goodbye once more to teary family members and friends and leaving all that they knew, John, Jen, and baby Noah headed down the road toward Charlotte, North Carolina. It was certain this time that this was where John was to minister, but this realization required his coming back to tune into God's instruction and direction for where he would best help other souls in need. A true calling indeed comes by listening and preparing yourself for wherever the adventure leads. It has been four prosperous years of John and Jen's ministry since they left us, but the heart that follows the call of God is blessed beyond belief.

I speak firsthand of this inspirational couple. I have ministered with them, and my family has been unforgettably enriched because this couple listened to the voice of God delivered through the courageous lady who confronted them.

Perhaps John expresses the Good News of the Bible so well because of the passion he carries in his heart to love, serve, follow, and stay connected with Jesus. The message to hear from his teachings is that even if we cannot see ourselves as in concert with God but are willing to hear His word anyway, God has an indescribable path ready for us. He will use each talent He has lavished upon us to prepare us for the glory of His kingdom. We are not often afforded idle time to discuss our paths, but when we do, John keeps his focus on the amazement he has for all the Lord has called and equipped this tireless servant to do!

Is there a challenge here for you to hear? Pray about what you have read today, and see if you become aware of anything that the still, small voice of the Spirit may be saying to you. Psalm 46:10 is the simplest explanation of how our soul is to hear: "Be silent, and know that I am God."

QUESTIONS TO BEGIN WITH

- How much time do we really spend listening for the voice of God in our lives? We all often talk to God, but do we stop long enough to hear an answer or to be given a direction to go?

- How have you heard God calling in your life?

- Has anyone been a voice for God in your life?

- What do you think God has equipped you to do to share a connection to the Gospel with others?

- Do you think God has a calling in mind for everyone? (Read 1 Corinthians 12 -31 to help you answer this – "One Body with Many Parts")

SCRIPTURES TO CONNECT TO

2 Thessalonians 3:5, Deuteronomy 13:1-4, Titus 2:11-12, Psalm 81: 10&13

Matthew 9:19, John 5:1-15 (Read this account of Jesus healing the lame man; our situations will not change until we desire to Hear the call to change our lives and attitudes!)

Personal Moments

Personal Moments

Chapter Three: Back to an Obedient Heart

A Connection to God's Heart – "Then God said, 'Let us make people in our own image, to be like ourselves. They will be masters over all life – the fish in the sea, the birds in the sky, and all the livestock, wild animals, and small animals.' So God created people in His own image; God patterned them after Himself; male and female, He created them." -Genesis 1: 26-27

What better place is there to start than at the literal creation of people? God's plan from the beginning was to connect Himself so personally with us that we were created to look like Him. Could any connection have tied us closer to heaven? In that beautiful garden we will pause to look at the only thing we were asked to do – listen.

Genesis is the book that tells the story of a wondrous new beginning. Here we encounter the first experiences of love, marriage, purity, and perfection. But as the saying goes, "There are two sides to every story." Mixed into the mystery of creation, God gave us humans the dynamic ability to choose the path our lives would take. So began the dark presence of temptation slipping in and testing the very ones who were created always to be with God. The honeymoon-like freshness of being surrounded in a garden utopia was jeopardized by actions that pass God's limits, called sin. When this sin entered the world, it separated us from God, but because God's love is endless, He works to restore our relationship with Him. He wants to make Himself known to us and continue to stay connected with all people who seek Him.

The story of the Man and the Woman in Eden:

Follow me if you will through the story of two people who were given life in the pristine garden called Eden. The whole earth is no longer formless or empty; creation is complete. God has deemed that all is done well (See Genesis 2:1-3). Adam and Eve are placed in the garden to tend and care for it. It was paradise – never before or never again to be duplicated! The couple enjoyed perfect weather, beautiful nature, and an incredible abundance of delicious food. But the most awesome thing of all that was given to them was the opportunity to walk every day with God. God blessed them with everything He had, only making one request: that they obey Him (see Genesis 2:8-17).

Right in the center of the garden were two trees. These particular trees were hard to resist. Only the most perfect fruit grew here! What was even more special and most tempting about the trees was the power they held. Contained in the forbidden branches was eternal life and access to the knowledge of good and evil. Who would not want a bite of that? That was the exact problem that Adam and Eve faced, and the sweet enticement of sin was presented to them. Now they wrestled with the temptation to give in to this desire to take what they thought God wanted to keep from them. This was tough. On the one hand, God had provided much for them, but on the other hand, that fruit sure did look good, and wouldn't the ability to know everything be rewarding? (See Genesis 3:1-3)

Their dilemma resulted in their choice to disobey what was asked of them. After taking the fruit and tasting it, they knew right away that something was wrong. Because they had made a rebellious choice, separation between the Spirit and the world occurred. When God appeared for daily fellowship with His people, He was alone. Adam and Eve could no longer walk with God freely. They were now separated. The connection that had started out to last forever was now broken (See Genesis 3:6-13).

The man and his wife knew what their actions had cost, and they wanted to be right with God again. Our behavior cannot be overlooked, but God wants to be with us so much that He offers us a way back through His forgiveness. When we take responsibility for our actions, God grants the way back into His heart.

Now we leave the garden, understanding how Adam and Eve reconnected back to God after such a costly meal! The garden was closed. They reaped the consequence of no longer having the privilege of living inside Eden. The consequence of sin is to live forever on the other side of paradise. The plush life of no work, no pain, and all of their needs instantly accommodated was over. They learned the valuable lesson that God means what He says, even if enforcing the consequences makes Him sad. Personally, I am grateful to have a God of character, justice, love, and mercy to connect to, even after we stray from His heart (see Genesis 3:14-24).

Our listening and obedience to God is always for our benefit. God does not want merely to order us around or keep things from us, but like a good parent, His intentions are to teach our hearts so we can live a life that is unshakeable. Listening to God's commands will keep us aware of our paths when temptations try to interfere and compromise our spiritual connection.

It is so important to God that we belong to Him. He has done the hard work and made a priceless promise to us. Meditate on the scripture found in Hebrews 8:10 and listen to what the Spirit says to you. "I will put my laws in their minds so they will understand them, and I will write them on their hearts so they will obey them. I will be their God and they will be my people." Isn't that what we want? Reach out and appreciate this lifeline thrown to us from heaven. My friends, one mistake does not have to dictate your future; turn around and walk with God again to the places to which only He can bring us. God sets standards to protect us from evil and harm, not to motivate our loyalty out of fear or obligation. Obedience actually frees us to enjoy life by returning the love we have been given to others. Even though God's commands may appear difficult, He gives them to us to bless us and spare the potential heartache that often our human eyes cannot detect. Human perspective is what keeps us from receiving what God really wants to give us – life with Him in Eden forever!

QUESTIONS TO BEGIN WITH

- Can you name any temptations that have tested your obedience to God or willingness to listen?

- Why do you think obedience to God matters?

- When our connection with God is weakened, what are some things we can do to reconnect? What did Adam and Eve do?

- Do you think a reconnection with God can be as strong as the first time we walked with God?

- Does God look at us differently after we have made a mistake?

- Challenge: Read the entire Garden of Eden account in Genesis 2 & 3. Note how unnoticed sin creeps in and affects our spiritual relationship with God.

SCRIPTURES TO CONNECT TO

Romans 6:23, 1 Peter 5:8, Luke 14:33, Galatians 2:16-21, Psalm 1:1, Galatians 6:7

Philippians 2:5-13, Matthew 25:14-30, John 19:1-11, Proverbs 1:23

Personal Moments

Personal Moments

Chapter Four: Back to a Changed Heart

A Connection to God's Heart – "But you are near, O Lord, and all your commands are true. I have known from my earliest days that your decrees never change. Look down upon my sorrows and rescue me, for I have not forgotten your law! Argue my case; take my side! Protect my life as you promised." -Psalm 119:151-154

For those of us who have begun to seek a relationship with God later in life, join me in looking back and recalling those first amazing encounters after you were introduced to Jesus as the Messiah. I can image that your heart felt fresh, joyful, reborn.... changed (as it was for me). The spirit of Christ that enters us provides us the reason to seek to be connected with everything this change offers. It doesn't matter whether a life has been one of a constant awareness of a Spiritual presence or not; it only matters that the change was made to gain this awareness now.

It is probably safe to suggest that moments of change present themselves all around us. Changes in life seem to be as certain as the gradual erosion of time. Any way you are comfortable considering it, change is nature's way of producing ways for our lives to become different with both positive and negative effects. Life itself is God's gift of continual change.

How many changes have already entered your world? Whirlwind emotions of upheaval, tragedy, and celebration have forever incorporated themselves into the hidden recesses of your heart. Change can be so prevalent that sometimes nothing feels normal. People, relationships, jobs, technology, and even the atmosphere seem to move at blinding speeds! These are the things on earth that cause us the most catastrophic change. But have you ever considered the eternal change the Holy Spirit offers us? The results as I understand them are quiet different. Natural disasters and traumatic trials are but brief dilemmas, but the choice between being with or without God forever is a choice that changes the eternity we will experience.

True to any decision for change, at some point we must face accountability. We look for someone or something on which to blame our pain or loss. When we describe any cataclysmic circumstance that leaves behind devastation, our first question is: why? Who is accountable in our spiritual journey, and who is asked to make these changes? Dear friend, who do you see in your mirror? Are we willing to accept the changed heart that is required to achieve a reconnection to God?

After this heavy dose of "that's the way it is," take comfort. Despite the fast-changing axis the world revolves on, the Bible teaches us two fabulous truths about the condition of change. First, God is changeless and certain. Second, our hearts remain closed if we do not seize chances for change. The change that the soul longs for is at the heart, which will fail us if we do not tend to it. A heart that knows not a spiritual change becomes hard, dark, bitter, and resentful. The light of a changed heart opens the way for love and joy to enter in. We cannot reach God without a change of heart and the resulting actions it brings. We are asked to succumb to the change that occurs from inside us, called repentance, which is realized when an outer lifestyle change called obedience is produced. Although this is a tough process, it is possible by God's grace.

My husband and father-in-law are avid fishermen, so they will appreciate the story about the "one that got away" – almost! In this case, the fish was not the subject of the story, but a man, Jonah, who wanted to escape what God told him to do, but God reeled him back in and helped Jonah change his heart.

Jonah's story:

How far do you think God will go to get our attention? Would you go to the lengths of our pal Jonah, inside a whale, deep within the sea before your ears perk up? Sadly, many of us must have a similarly dramatic event to grab our attention. We have much in common with Jonah and his deep sea ride. For starters, he knew God, and many of us claim also to know Him. Jonah also believed his way was better that the Lord's. Does any of this sound familiar yet? See if you can picture yourself in Jonah's predicament as we once again travel back long ago to shed some light on our lives today!

On a dock in a crowded fishing town in the middle of the night, Jonah was given a task that he had no intention of completing. He boarded a boat, but that was as far as he would go to obey God. God told him he was to preach the good news of salvation for all men in the terribly wicked city of Nineveh. Having none of this, Jonah placed himself on a ship, setting sail for a land hundreds of miles in the opposite direction. Did God notice? You bet he did! God took so much notice that He allowed this fisherman to catch more then he had planned.

Rough storms, cold winds, and a water-filled boat could be enough to scare anyone, and even more so when you know that you are the cause. Jonah knew he could not let his crew endure any more fear because of his mistake. Not knowing what else to do, Jonah quickly explained that he was the source of God's anger and he begged the men to cast him overboard. Over he went, bags, baggage, and all! With the sea satisfied and finally calm, Jonah's journey to a changed heart began. Many of us who spent any amount of time in Sunday school know what comes next. Jonah was gobbled up by a huge fish! Why would someone who knew God want to end up here?

After three days of prayer and conversation with God, our seafaring friend was ready to follow the original plan. Back on to dry land, the big fish spit up a renewed Jonah who wasted not a moment and traveled straight away to the city of Nineveh. He told the people his story, and because it was recited with a changed heart back in agreement with God, the city was spared. God's love and mercy was able to reign in the lives of those transformed people, along with a much changed and forever wiser Jonah.

This was indeed a whale of a tale, but it provides a word of warning to us all. If needed, God will get us alone so that He can deal with the condition of our heart and bring it back to where it needs to be: in line with His.

QUESTIONS TO BEGIN WITH

- Is there something you would like to run away from? Is it possible to run from God?

- What are the escape routes you have planned out?

- What things in life have changed for you, both positively and negatively? Have you experienced any benefits from the changes your life has brought you?

- Are there changes yet to be made in your life? Are you willing to allow God the opportunity to be part of the decision process?

- Why did Jonah need to drop to the depths of the ocean to convince him to change his mind back to God? What has been your bottom-of-the-sea moment, if any?

SCRIPTURES TO CONNECT TO

Job 10:1, 2 Corinthians 1:4, Jonah 2:1-10, Psalm 119:115, Mark 6:7-11, Galatians 5:24

1 Corinthians 10:13, 1 Peter 4:1-5, 1 Samuel 12:15, Isaiah 59:2, Jeremiah 3:22

Personal Moments

Personal Moments

Chapter Five: Back to a Steadfast Heart

A Connection to God's Heart – "The steadfast love of the Lord never ceases, His mercies never come to an end; they are new every morning: great is thy faithfulness." -Lamentations 3:22-23

Great is thy faithfulness… that is a beautiful promise indeed. Just as beautiful is when we understand that true steadfastness comes from the attitude in which we live and express our life. Go down a few more lines in your Bible and take intentional note of verse 25 in chapter 3 of Lamentations. "The Lord is wonderfully good to those who wait for Him and seek Him." Can you imagine a life spent knowing that you could rest safely and be genuinely happy in the goodness of the Lord? Mind boggling, yes; impossible… no way! If we retain a clear picture of why Jesus died for us and focus on what He is doing in heaven, which is preparing a place we can live with Him forever because He loves us, then we are simply free to live out our time here on earth with peace and joy.

Even in the midst of such great knowledge, we still face the test of day-to-day living. How can we even hope that the faithfulness of God will be enough? Each person must find the answer individually, but I can share what I believe to be the truth. Each new day, God supplies the freshness of abundant opportunities and the gift of time to set our feet on the right path. Best of all is the renewed showering of God's loving kindness filled with the strength we need to succeed and accomplish more then we ever thought possible. As we visualize each new day as the blessing it is, offer back to God thanksgiving for the assurance of His protective presence in the care of our lives.

I am convinced that the ability to abide in the steadfast love of God comes from our desire to be disciplined enough to learn His ways. That is what the test of life seems to come down to: living my way or living God's way. You can measure your steadfast intentions by the way you answer this question: would I allow anything to happen in my life without God's permission? Remember that God created us out of deep love and the desire to build a relationship with us.

Memories of My Mother-in-Law's Love:

Time is the test by which we determine something's value and worth. For example, if a life can endure 50 years of marriage, the loss of a baby, heartaches of precious family members, the struggles of raising 10 children, and life at the center of love for 25 grandchildren and still sing the praises of the Lord at the end of it, it was well done.

The Word of God has been the source of light in my life for more than 15 years now, but the numerous lessons that it teaches take a lifetime to retain. Most of what I know about a spiritual journey I learned from what I have seen in one special life. The lessons modeled for me through my mother-in-law's life are tools I treasure, use, and apply. The reason they are of such immeasurable value is because they are grounded in the steadfast pursuit of doing things God's way.

I can remember very few days that there was not a smile on her face or a kind word to share. What did she see, exactly? I am sure that she saw God's mercies every morning. In fact, one of the songs she sang was, "I will sing of the mercies of the Lord forever, I will sing, I will sing." And she sang! For the 22 years I knew her, she sang this song to her grown children, her grandchildren, and anyone else who would listen. Fortunately, I took the time to listen to her and have been blessed beyond words by her song of salvation.

This steadfast conviction in believing and living God's word spanned several decades. My mother-in-law's life was so Christ-centered that she believed the same principles from the 1960s until God took her home in 2008! God's word was her joy, and His ways were never out of style. I look back with so much pleasure as I think about our conversations together. We discussed Jesus, marriage, children, and life as women, and her advice and direction were always the same: "Well, scripture says…" She would then smile and repeat God's side of the story, sweetly or sternly, if need be. Although she could be stern, she was never unloving. She so desperately wanted everyone to hear the stories of truth that she taught them to her family, praying that they would pass these truths on.

One of my less attractive traits is my tendency to whine at times. I would mention to my mother-in-law more often than she would have liked how I wished that Jesus would just come back. This upset her, and she reminded me to think before expressing such a desire, since we need to think about those who did not yet have a relationship with Jesus and would not have the chance to be with Him in heaven if He came then. As Christian believers we are taught that when Jesus returns, He will only take those who have accepted Him to heaven, leaving everyone else to face damnation. She believed that God did His job and we should do ours. She arose every day dressed in the armor of the Lord and did the right things He wanted her to do. (see Ephesians 6: 10-20)

Every prayer Mom uttered was offered in full confidence that her God would answer it. It didn't matter how great or impossible her requests seemed or whether she would still be on earth to see the result. She knew her prayers were heard and would be answered. She clung to Bible verses as if God were right there in the room, speaking with her face to face. Through her steadfast prayers, two passages of scripture outlined all she needed to know about the power of prayer. Matthew 18:20, "If two or three are gathered together because they are mine, I am among them," and Philippians 4:6-7, "Don't worry about anything; instead, pray about everything. Tell God what you need, and thank Him for all He has done."

These acts were exactly what I saw her do over all those years. My mother-in-law met regularly with her best friend and prayer partner, and for more than 30 years lifted up the needs of others to the Lord, individually by name. What a dynamic force they were in the heavenly realms as they rattled the gates of hell! Can you imagine the time and dedication it took to be that committed to a love that deep? They knew in their hearts that God does not ignore our prayers (Psalm 9:12) and were convinced of His provincial authority on every issue. It did not matter to these ladies if the issue in question was significant or minor; the duo remained connected, living in line with God's will and not human wisdom.

When Mom closed her eyes for the last time on a cold February morning, she closed them in peace, because her lifetime of sincere prayers had brought about great miracles (James 5:16). A steadfast life doesn't leave room for guessing, and my dear mother-in-law lived her life showing others that she believed what she knew!

How do we get back to a steadfast heart and an unshakable conviction? Try these three choices that I have learned to be the elements of steadfast conviction. One, confess our sinful ways and asked to be freed. Two, submit to God's will and not our agenda. Doing this allows God to invade our life. Three, communicate with God. Simply pray. Get alone and tell God what we need, and then trust in Him.

Being steadfast is a sacrifice. Energy, time, and thought are required to make each decision we face. It is imperative that we prepare ourselves to clash with the sensitivity of society. A cavalier existence will not survive. We must see black and white, letting anything go that is gray. If we call that which is good to be bad and call what is bad to be good, how do we know on what side of an issue we stand? That which is temporarily pleasing will cause us to change our view daily. But if we remain steadfast on the side of God, we will know that nothing changes, and we will have no fear of having the rug pulled out from under us when the next popular thing comes along. The act of guarding our minds takes effort, and it can sometimes even be painful. It may even call for us to sacrifice a certain group of friends, habits, addictions, types of entertainment, style of dress, or even style of living. Each of us ought to make sure that everything that penetrates our lives supports what we believe. Having a foot in both the secular and spiritual worlds is a dangerous balancing act. If we are to live as Christians and followers of Christ, then our character can be only that of Jesus. We are here among our fellow people, just where Jesus loves to be, and as we have read in the gospel, the human thrives as God challenges and elevates us to the heights of heaven!

Steadfast love relentlessly pursues what is good and will not be moved from it. If we betray that type of commitment and comply with what is easy, then we are not steadfast, but easily swayed. No man alive could change the mind of my mother-in-law into believing that we can negotiate God's instruction. It is a conscious choice to walk the path less traveled; that is why so few of us take it. Wide roads seem more pleasant because they are paved, with room for all and tolerance for what is harmful. Take a lesson from those who did not side with what brings fleeting happiness only for a moment just because it appeared pleasing.

I'd like to offer this encouragement to you as it was offered to me. A steadfast heart will make its home in us when we praise, repent, appreciate, and yearn. Pray for the truths of the Holy Spirit. Let me repeat: pray for the truths of the Holy Spirit and find the meaning in the message. Lastly, use this scripture whenever you are losing the grip of a steadfast spirit in your life: "Love the Lord your God with all your heart, all your soul, all your mind, and all your strength" (Deuteronomy 6:5). By making this scripture the prayer of our hearts, we can be brought back again to the type of love God is worthy to receive.

QUESTIONS TO BEGIN WITH

- Is your heart connected in a steadfast relationship to God? Do we twist our relationship with God to be what we want it to be, or do we proceed in assurance to accomplish what pleases God?

- What are the promises given in Lamentations 3:22-23? How can these promises encourage us?

- How steadfast or unshakeable are you in the things you believe? Does God hold your attention or does the world's preference dictate our decisions?

- What specifically have you remained steadfast in within your spiritual relationship? For example, you may maintain steadfastness in prayer, your spiritual journey, parenting, entertainment choices, and friendships based on beliefs. What have been some results that you can look back on?

- Micah 6:8 tells us exactly what God is looking for us to be steadfast in. Read these words, "He has showed you, O man, what is good. And what does the Lord require of you? Too act justly and to love mercy and to walk humbly with your God."

- Why might this passage be challenging?

- What are the things the Lord has given you personally to sing about?

SCRIPTURES TO CONNECT TO

Luke (1:50 & 12:4), Hosea 2:19, Matthew 12:35, Psalm 27:1, Isaiah 41:10, Job 19:25

Proverbs 20:11, 1 Samuel 15:22, Romans 5:3-5, Jeremiah 17:7, 1 John 3:2

Personal Moments

Personal Moments

Chapter Six: Back to a Willing Heart

A connection to God's Heart - When it was clear that we couldn't persuade Him, we gave up and said, "The will of the Lord be done." -Acts 21:14

Can we really hope to know God's will for our lives? How many times has that question rattled in our minds wanting to be answered? The internal conflict arises when it is not a truthful answer we sincerely seek to gain, but a less painful way out of our situations. Why do we attempt to persuade God that our way is better than his? Letting go of our strong will and allowing God to work in us is the only way we achieve what is best for us. As God exposes His heart to us through His Word, we come to understand that His promises are sure and certain.

Getting close to God sometimes seems out of reach, so we often give up. The magnitude of our worldliness hinders our reception of the answer we seek. Perhaps we take a passive role and are just waiting for God to reveal something of Himself to us. In reality, He already has, but if we are bystanders in this relationship, we will not see these things right away. The will of God for His people is available. Each one of our lives is of unique interest and is individually vested in by our Creator. Through study of the scriptures, we can come to recognize that God had a plan for our lives before we were even conceived, love is the highest goal that we can achieve, and God equips us with all we need to live a life pointing to Him. None are excluded in these truths; God desires us to be part of accomplishing wonderful things. When we commit our work to the Lord, we cannot fail! With God, the work is not impossible because we are guaranteed success. Notice I did not say the work is easy, but that we are promised prosperity, which is even better. We can rest completely assured and expect something marvelous as we move forward in faith (Proverbs 16:3).

Let's refresh ourselves with the beautiful, ageless story of Queen Esther. We will enter the story in the palace of a King. In the book of Esther, chapter 4:13-17 reveals how this simple life was used and elevated to the highest privilege as Esther obtained special favor with a king. This particular favor came about at the perfect time. Her steadfastness to the will of God brought safety to her Jewish people. Esther offered her life willingly to the timing of the Lord, to be used as He wished. The purpose of her life came to a climax in such a way that the tale spans a lifetime! You will not regret one moment of being swept up into her story. Each one of us has been designed to carry a piece of Esther's willing heart and spirit as we yield our lives to God's perfect plan; that is the first key to opening our story to our heavenly King.

Human ethics has taught us much about completing tasks and complying agreeably with what is being asked of us to do. Willingness does not even factor into the equation; we do what we are told. There are numerous examples of how obligation motivates our actions in response. Why is it that we struggle so hard to listen when God asks the same of us? I would conclude that we struggle probably because we cannot fool God. He created our hearts; therefore He already sees what is inside. It takes more than good deeds to convince God that it is His will we long to give ourselves to. A willing heart is one in which nothing stands between you and God, especially personal preference of how we think things should proceed.

A touchy topic that I think is worthy of mentioning is change. Change will contribute a huge part to the way we will interact with God as He works His will into our daily living. Undoubtedly, some changes that will occur are painful and difficult. Stepping out of our comfort zones and examining our lifestyle choices, bad habits, and negative attitudes make all of us feel uncomfortable. We will not willingly change what is second nature and familiar; stubbornness wants to keep us right where we are. It takes work and an openness to surrender the baggage of our life to God. God promises that we will not face what we cannot handle. It is comforting to know that if God brings us to it, He will bring us through it.

Our knowledge of who we think God is will not prompt us to live a life that will bring Him glory. As this chapter's opening scripture verse illuminates, there is no way to persuade Jesus to conform to our ways; instead we ought to allow Him to elevate us to His standards. We must be willing to listen quietly, letting the spirit of God speak and free us to follow the direction Christ inspires.

The poem, *Little Ewe*, which was introduced to you at the outset of this book, is about surrendering mind, body, and soul to the will of God. This submission comes from a very private place in the soul, because it goes against everything you want to do and devotes your life totally to God. Ultimate battles of the will churn when your heart is so torn between your desired destination and the direction in which you are asked to travel. Can you grasp being given a divine direction straight from the heart of God to yours and instead of proceeding, you sit down? The author of the poem knew that place too, and understood she needed God's direction before she could move. Our approach of folding our arms in protest, digging our heels deeply into the very ground He created, and resisting to respond to the will of His call eventually leaves us alone and fearful. God's love enters in to provide courage, strength, and the gentle urging needed to accomplish any task. The Spirit of God carries us through each and every valley we cross. God doesn't say He will take away our turmoil, but He promises to deliver us safely to the other side of our trials in peace. So, just like the little lamb, a woman named Rita took timid steps back to her Heavenly Father. A lot of her journey was bravely shared in her poem. It is with permission that I share the rest of the story with you.

Rita's story:

My sister-in-law, Rita, poured her heart out into a poem, and I am so blessed that she has agreed to share it with all of us. Rita has one of the biggest and most giving hearts there is. She is the type of person you can depend on consistently. Her burden is often overwhelming, but she is generous both with her time and with physical help. In every situation, Rita devotes whatever it takes to get the job done. Over the years, her profession has been of service to others, including 14 years of work in the family restaurant business and over 12 years as a nanny and senior care giver. In every situation, she can be found serving others! If someone needs help with holiday party setup, Rita is there. If someone is having a baby, Rita is there. If you need a babysitter, help painting your house, or a friend to hang out with, Rita is there. She loves others with such an open heart that it was hard to image that she was struggling to accept God's will. Just because one grows up in a home where God's word is shared, Jesus' example taught, and the songs of the Spirit sung, one may not necessarily walk right along with it.

When God knocks on the door of a heart, we eventually open it. Slowly, we inch closer to His plea to "Come follow Me." Before we realize it, the old ways that displease the Lord are abandoned, and we seek new thoughts, but this is not an easy or quick process, albeit a worthy one. As we witness this transformation of our loved ones, we stand in awe of their character and strength. That is what we all saw in Rita. The journey she began taught her all about God's grace, and she traded everything she knew for a new relationship with the Lord. This became a life of total trust in what was yet to be explored.

As situations presented themselves, I watched and listened as Rita made decisions both in her personal and professional life. She is a lot like her mother; both make choices in a slow, deliberate, and sure manner. Rita does not act upon impulse. There is a special peace and calm about her that comes only from being surrounded with the will of God. Of course, she has faced decisions that ended with one answer – a tough one. From the small changes to the big, life-altering choices, Rita moved along with God's will for her life. Some were easy and some were not.

In her professional work as a nanny, Rita naturally assumed she would be with a family she worked for until little Gabby started the first grade. Rita and Gabby connected to each other and their years together were enjoyable for them. However, God's will for Rita was different from her plans. When Gabby was four years old, God began to put it on Rita's heart that she would be moving on. Rita resisted, unable to believe that the time to leave had come. Her heart was heavy, but God's voice said, "No, come this way, little ewe." Even as she gave her notice, her heart hurt, but she knew it was what God wanted.

A few years later, Rita once again faced a life-changing direction in her personal life. Learning that her mom was terminally ill, Rita knew there was precious little time left. Overtaken by many emotions and not knowing what to do or how to deal with this knowledge, she lived confused, hurt, and scared. In the middle of all the family upset, Rita was told that the apartment she had been renting for more than 20 years was going to be demolished. How could she possibly find a place to live when it was the last thing she could focus on? The stress was terrible for her. Then God impressed upon her that she would be moving home. Again she resisted, even with the open invitation from her father. After being on her own for so many years, moving home was a hard concept to accept. God's voice again called out the familiar words, "No, come this way, little ewe." Rita made the decision to go home because it was God's will, and at the same time had to come to terms with God's will in her mother's life.

Even in the most unthinkable situations, God's words spoke of his mercy and pointed her towards His throne of grace. She knew she had to proceed in the will of God for her life. Now she needed to let her mom return home to the Lord. In moments of pain, clear understanding came to her. I asked Rita how she could deal with the sadness this event brought, and without hesitation, the answer for her was an amazingly simple statement, "Because I know God is there."

Rita relies on the words expressed in Psalm 23. Verse 4 reads, "Even though I walk through the dark valley of death I will not be afraid, for you are close beside me." Definitely there is something in these words we all can find comfort in. The world changes, but God is with us always. We are never trapped in the hard times of a situation; by staying close in the will of God, we get all the way through our trials. Wouldn't it be nice if we were always excited about following God's will and not our own? Of course it is just not that easy! How do we get back to the beginning from our furthest point of frustration? Get on our knees, one prayer at a time. Isn't that the best place to start? Believe me; Jesus is waiting to hear from you.

QUESTIONS TO BEGIN WITH

- Define what a willing heart connected to God means to you?

- Can you recall personal situations you willingly allowed God to walk you through? (See Psalm 23)

- Attempt your own Psalm such as *Little Ewe*. Share the situations that are hard for you to emerge from. Perhaps a fear, addiction, or unresolved pain is holding you from experiencing the freedom of God's love and goodness.

- Can you think of an issue for which you sought total control instead of the guidance of the Lord? Did you get the result you had hoped for? Did you find yourself needing to go back to the beginning and do it all again with the support of the Holy Spirit?

- "...God's own people, Israel. He cared for them with a true heart and led them with skillful hands" (Psalm 78:72). Meditate on this scripture. God is King of the entire universe, yet we are loved individually. Place your name in Israel's spot, record some moments in which God has skillfully given you care. Where are the places to which God's hands have led you? Thank Him for his willful and desiring heart to be connected to you.

SCRIPTURES TO CONNECT TO

Hebrews 10:33 & 4:15, 2 Corinthians 12:10 & 1:3-4, Timothy 2:10, 1 Peter 3:8

Hosea 6:3, Esther 4:13-17, Exodus 20:1-17, Proverbs 5:1-6, 1 Kings 3: 5-14

Personal Moments

Personal Moments

Chapter Seven: Back to a Teachable Heart

A Connection to God's Heart – "I call to you, to all of you! I am raising my voice to all people. How naive you are! Let me give you common sense. O foolish ones, let me give you understanding. Listen to me! For I have excellent things to tell you. Everything I say is right, for I speak the truth and hate every kind of deception. My advice is wholesome and good. There is nothing crooked or twisted in it. My words are plain to anyone with understanding, clear to those who want to learn. Choose my instruction rather than silver, and knowledge over pure gold. For wisdom is far more valuable than rubies. Nothing you desire can be compared to it." -Proverbs 8:4-11

With the numerous demands placed on our time each day, we wonder how one more thing can be crammed in. The mere thought of learning something new can make some people cringe. But there is a lot of good news about the incredible mysteries God wants to open to our world. God says that we can take Him at His word. Proverbs 8:4-11 lays the foundation for this message as we begin to turn back toward what we have strayed from: a yearning to learn. The most exciting piece of knowledge I have obtained is that God has excellent things He wants to tell us! What are these excellent things? It will do us well to explore the chapter's opening Bible verse and invest our beginning moments in preparing our hearts for the things God wants to teach us. Let's investigate what we can glean from the above passage so far. Re-read it as you keep in mind that any worthwhile process seems harder before it gets easier; we have to want to learn and allow good knowledge into our heart.

God Himself extends the following so that we can learn: common sense, understanding, truth, wholesome good advice, plain words, and valuable wisdom. We protect these treasures of teaching when we are diligent in our response by hating what is deceptive and rejecting the folly of the foolish and by refusing to heed the instruction to which nothing here on earth can compare. A recurring theme throughout our lives that we must grasp is that no one can be taught if they do not want to be, and every day we can open our eyes to new possibilities.

A person's knowledge comes not from all they know but from what they are willing to remember. How many of us have heard our parents repeat the same lectures over and over again? Why is it necessary for them to repeat themselves? A heart must be moved before it will listen. The same is true in our relationship with God. He talks, but unless we are willing to believe, our heart refuses to remember what He has been teaching us.

The Apostle Paul

This rugged and untamed man of God is the perfect specimen for us to research briefly in this point. Paul was not always a man of God. Please indulge me as I recount the basic story of this apostle and the day he met Jesus.

Paul was passionate, fierce, and intelligent. He was educated by the best rabbis of the land. A Jew by birth, Paul was born into wealth and also had Roman citizenship. Jewish law and religion were his expert fields of study, so it can be said that Paul was a man who had been educated. He had yet to learn, however, who Jesus was – the King of the Jews who was killed by the very Romans with whom he shared a connection.

Notorious as a vicious persecutor of Christ's teachings, Paul went on a rampage to rid the world of these religious beliefs. With the word of the law as his shield, he set to cause pain, death, and suffering at any cost to see justice done. Many Christians died by his hand, including a gentle and much loved servant of God named Stephen. Seemingly unstoppable, Paul had no idea that the lesson he would be taught was one that would change his heart forever.

Having set off on what he had planned to be his most destructive crusade, Paul's story took a dynamic turn. Jesus taught Paul who He is, personally. Imagine, if you will, galloping on your trusted horse, wildly heading down a dusty road as rocks and pebbles explode beneath you, thrown in every direction. Nothing stands in the way between you and your destination. This describes

Paul's state and probably even his thoughts as he traveled on the dirt road straight to Damascus.

As he neared his destination, a light more brilliant than he had ever seen beamed down on Paul. Before he knew it, he was on the ground, totally blinded from the light. A voice Paul had never heard before spoke like thunder. Calling him by name, the booming voice asked only one question: "Saul! Saul! Why are you persecuting me?" Paul could only breathe out the phrase, "Who are you?"

Jesus told his persecutor who He was and what He wanted. Then Jesus commanded, "Go and do what I say. For Saul is my chosen instrument to take my message to the Gentiles and to kings as well as to the people of Israel." Known as Saul before he met Jesus, Paul is sometimes referred to today as the Lion of the Lord. Paul received a new name, which illustrates that we cannot be touched by the hand of God and expect to remain the way we were. God's reaches our heart so that He can teach it.

The most powerful letters and lessons that the church teaches today have been penned by the hand of he who had been the vilest of men. Paul declares himself the worst of men until the day Jesus met him on the road and taught him who He was, changing his nature for the rest of his days on earth. Paul's life story provides us with so much passion from which we can draw strength and knowledge. He stopped at no cost to pursue his purpose, and once he was convinced of Jesus, he proclaimed His name as Messiah throughout all the regions of the world. Paul's conversion from a man who never walked with Jesus to a humbled servant who clung to the work of the cross is what the power of salvation should mean to every person.

I share this story straight from the book of Acts in the first ten chapters in order to illustrate this magnificent conversion to God. Paul's story sheds light on the message that we will hear when we are willing to hear it.

Praise God that He will do what it takes to get our attention. My prayer is that our sight will be illuminated like Paul's, and that we may learn abundantly more each day. May God continue to be gracious and continue to help us to always be reachable so that our hearts will stay teachable.

QUESTIONS TO BEGIN WITH

- Have you been taught anything new spiritually recently?

- From our chapter's main Bible verse, what are some of the things God wants to tell us? List some of them and pray that you may gain fresh understanding.

- Challenge yourself to read more about the life of Paul and especially through the book of Acts note what he was taught.

- What is the weakest trait that keeps your heart from being teachable? Do you know what you may want to ask God to help you work on? Some examples include being too set in our habits, being too busy to change, or failing to see the point of even trying to explore new ways.

•   Remember some of the wonderful things God has already taught you and offer them back as praise!

SCRIPTURES TO CONNECT TO

Exodus 19:16-20, 1 Timothy 4:1-13, 1 Peter 1:7, Romans 1:20, Hosea 14:9

Proverbs 1: 8-9 & 2:1-9, Genesis 44:15, Matthew 6 (what we are to be taught)

Personal Moments

Personal Moments

Chapter Eight: Back to a Serving Heart

A Connection to God's Heart – "Is there any encouragement from belonging to Christ? Any comfort from His love? Any fellowship together in the Spirit? Are your hearts tender and sympathetic? Then make me truly happy by agreeing wholeheartedly with each other, loving one another, and working together with one heart and purpose.... Your attitude should be the same that Christ Jesus had. Though he was God, He did not demand and cling to His rights as God. He made Himself nothing; He took the humble position of a slave and appeared in human form." -Philippians 2:1-2 & 2:5-7

Unity through humility is how we are all to be joined with Christ. Service is the essence of effective Christian living. With the acts of service Jesus Himself performed, He again turns the world's thinking over on its head. Isn't it a sign of great achievement in life to have others serve us? However, the message the Prince of Heaven came with was not a popular one; He challenged us to view life not motivated by obtaining servants, but by being a servant. If our intention is to carry the attitude of Christ, than we are accountable to do as He has shown. God's highest goal for His people is for them to participate in others' lives as selfless beings and not to isolate themselves in a self-centered world.

Jesus paid the cost of leaving heaven to live among those who would reject Him, physically hurt Him, betray Him, and even walk away from Him. That didn't matter; He loved them anyway and served always! The most beautiful image that plays in my mind is the vision of a King taking off his glorious crown and putting on instead the sacrificial towel of a humble slave. However, the best of the story is yet to come. Jesus was so compelled to model how far we should go in serving one another that He performed the task of a slave. In the Gospel of John 13:1-17, we encounter Jesus washing the feet of the disciples, the very ones He called to follow Him.

Would we be able to do what we have not yet seen done? Jesus knew the difficulty of this task. The Spirit of God played a great role in demonstrating service to others with the motivation to gain nothing. We are taught to use our whole body as a tool in doing what is right so that we can give ourselves completely to God (Romans 6:12-14). The connection between our hearts and God's is most strengthened when we are serving Him and those He loves.

Undeniably, this is not a casual commitment. Selfless kindness extended to all people is what a service-led life demands. When the hours are long, the work excruciating, and the pay nothing and yet we still serve, then we are serving as Christ. Serving as the Father has loved us allows us to understand the full meaning of the call of Jesus. "Come, be my disciple." Will we hear it or reject it? Will we step up and step out to make another's comfort our priority? (Matthew 9:57-62)

Nan's story:

The following is a wonderful story that will leave each one of us motivated and inspired. Although the principles demonstrated in this story can be found in any New Testament gospel where selfless love is learned, this story is about a modern-day woman who, like Jesus, was compelled by compassion. As most people, Nan valued knowledge and the concept of a spiritual journey, but it was not until her heart strings were pulled for her sister was she ready to answer a servant's call that was placed unexpectedly in her path. Would she find a way around it or would she call on Jesus to help her over this mountainous task? Let's explore from the beginning this story of the glorious gift poured out on the life of another.

Nan was my mother-in-law's sister. As the oldest of six children, my mother-in-law was 16 years older than Nan. Mom was extremely close with her siblings. Before their mother's death in 1988, Nan was experiencing an awkward time, being young in her marriage, raising three children, and trying to function at her job. She was not able to provide as much care to her mother as her siblings were. My mother-in-law had older children and was available during school hours to commute to

Philadelphia to care for their ailing mother, but Nan felt overwhelmed, and instead of tending to her mother, focused on raising her family. Of course, as time goes on, we learn more of life's lessons than we ever thought we could learn! She now understands better how God works in our lives and that He will lead us to where He wants us to be.

After the passing of their mother, Nan spent a lot of time with her sister, reaching out to her for support as Nan continued to build the foundation of a Christian home for her family. In her eyes, her sister Betty was the perfect choice for a role model. At the start, Betty provided the advice that Christ had to be put first. My mother-in-law told her that Jesus had to be her everything, because the Lord does not play second fiddle in any situation.

Betty enjoyed watching Nan grow in her spiritual journey. Both women have very loving, gentle spirits, and when they were together everyone could see the wonderful love between them. During the last 15 years they had together they organized family gatherings, summer camping trips, numerous road trips, time at Nan's Cape May shore house, and many, many cups of coffee at Betty's kitchen table. Nan and her family were part of Mom's daily life, and her children loved her like a grandmother.

Nan always had an interest in babies and childbirth, and she sought advice about becoming a doula, a woman who tends to the baby and mother during the delivery process. A labor and delivery doula is different from a midwife in that she is an advocate for the family, ensuring that the mother has the type of birth experience closest to what she expected. A postpartum doula helps the family adjust once the baby is home. Over the three to nine weeks after a birth, the new mom is afforded time to rest and is able to grow accustomed to tending to the newest family member.

My mother-in-law knew that Nan would be a great doula. Nan had the opportunity over the course of 12 years to work with several clients. She was truly starting to embrace the direction God was leading her to follow. Her family has grown; her children are now getting married, moving out, and attending college. There is now even a beautiful baby granddaughter for her to love! Although her life is busy, Nan is definitely heading in the direction she felt she should go. She even decided to go to work for a woman whose own doula business was growing.

Then Mom got sick. Of course, as her sister, Nan was worried. Mom was concerned that she would have to go to the hospital and asked Nan for help. You can understand that it takes a special person to be present during the night watch; Nan was the girl for the job! She functioned well during the late hours, being able to maintain a pleasant atmosphere while helping out in the morning. My mother-in-law entered the hospital the Tuesday night before Thanksgiving and did not return home to stay until February 18. Someone was by Mom's side every day and every night. Most of the time her daughter Betty Ann and her sister Nan sat by her side, since she so needed them as advocates. The rest of us watched by, listening and doing the things asked of us to do for Mom's dignity and comfort.

Nan would move to three different hospitals with Mom before this chapter of their story ended. In the last hospital, they were told that no one could stay overnight. Although unhappy, the family complied with the rules, remembering that God is good. Luckily, Nan did get to stay the first night and every night thereafter. She had calmly spoken to the woman in charge at the hospital and explained the situation. Mom had her family around her the entire time, thanks to people like Nan who spoke up for patients who can't speak for themselves. It was amazing to me to observe the care each member of this family gave to someone we all deeply loved beyond words. This love filtered down to each branch of the family tree. Mom's siblings were there almost every day of the week, as were countless friends and neighbors. Among the memories I will cherish dearly are three defining moments that are burned forever in my heart. The first moment is my mother-in-law's personal interaction with her own husband, children, and grandchildren. Later, someone lauded Nan for maintaining a fluttering presence in the room; we knew she was there, but she never interrupted anyone's visits or eavesdropped during personal conversations. She was never intrusive as she tended to her sister's every need. The next memories are the times I sat alone with Mom, thanking her for all she had done in my life. The last moment in my memory is my favorite, the one that ties the whole experience together and sealed for me the ultimate act of unconditional service and charity to another human being. I witness Nan's courage to remain devoted to Mom, and this observation still strikes me whenever I think about it. What a gift of humanity Nan was to her sister! Nan never complained, even when the cost to her presented pressure on her own health, husband, children, and career. She missed holidays, school events, and simple daily family life. But the understanding and support that came from her husband and children encouraged her to continue as she did.

Her love flowed from one woman to another, almost like it was her time to assume responsibility. What she could not do all those years ago for her mother she now lavished on her sister! This love embodies what my lifetime memory of Nan and her sister will be. Hours before my mother-in-law passed away, Nan had washed her beautifully and was rubbing lotion on her feet. This action blew me away! I wondered how the act of rubbing lotion on her feet would matter now, but I learned that a serving heart does not stop until God says we are done. Only a few days ago, I learned that right at the moment of my mother-in-law's death, Nan had again performed the same actions as before. While caring the basin of soapy warm water to the sink, Nan's sister took her last earthly breath. Mom met her Savior with the soles of her feet washed, with someone who loved her pouring out the servant water! Despite all the intimate care Nan gave, my mother-in-law's homecoming into heaven was meant just for her, privately meeting with her God.

I am left forever changed through observing Nan's service to my mother-in-law. All I can manage to say is, thank you, Nan! Praise be to God who enables those to serve with the genuine heart of Himself.

QUESTIONS TO BEGIN WITH

- How does God make it possible for us to love and serve others selflessly?

- Has there been a time in your life when you were the receipt of someone's special care during a rough time? What made that gift of nurture so special?

- Is there a better understanding of what a servant truly is? Write a few words describing the qualities of caregivers and of those who offer their services to benefit others.

- Is your heart open to being a servant of Christ? It may be uncomfortable to bear, but I encourage us all to look inside our hearts and ask God to show us obstacles that are hindering us.

- Recall a story (such as the story of Nan, which is so personal to me) that you might like to record, and ask God to help you do it. Seeing the wonderful potential in others inspires us to want to know exactly what it is and how to obtain it for ourselves. Do you agree? What do you think people want in their lives?

SCRIPTURES TO CONNECT TO

John 1:26-28, Acts 7:55-56, 1 Corinthians 2:9, Romans 14:18, Proverbs 12:16-18

1 Peter 4:11, Exodus 23:24, Matthew 5:44 & 7:12, Isaiah 33:15-16, Psalm 103:6

Personal Moments

Personal Moments

Chapter Nine: Back to a Focused Heart

A Connection to God's Heart – "I am warning you ahead of time, dear friends, so that you can watch out and not be carried away by the errors of these wicked people. I don't want you to lose your own secure footing. But grow in the special favor and knowledge of our Lord and Savior Jesus Christ." -2 Peter 3:17-18

It is not difficult to get knocked off course, is it? Before we even see it coming, our vision can be blurred and our focus can become unclear. Compromising values to impress those we don't even know, chasing after prestige, sacrificing the integrity of our relationships, and emulating the examples of corrupt people, we may find ourselves asking how this could possibly happen. Didn't we have it all together? Weren't we the ones in control of our lives? Where did we go wrong?

Joshua 24:15 may add some insight for us: "Choose today whom you will serve... But for me and my family, we will serve the Lord." This straightforward verse offers instruction under no uncertain terms where our focus should be. Wouldn't it be helpful to realize what is clearly at the core of our homes? Do the rules of the world dominate us, or do we have secure footing on solid ground?

Many distractions are waiting to blindside us. For me, culprits include frustration, fatigue, and the simple feeling of having had enough! When those emotions run at their peak intensity, humanly speaking, I am toast. Any one of us can find that our focus is instantly diverted by the consuming power of these forces. If you find yourself chasing your tail and following after the wrong things, stop, breathe, and look right back to Jesus. Although this seems a simple procedure, it took me 38 years to master it, but it brings me immense strength, and I love it! It is better to identify what has our lives in turmoil so we can deal with it by finding time alone with God. I have asked Him very recently to give me a clear focus in my life concerning my marriage and my growing children, and He has. Everything that has become tangled like a ball of string for more years than I care to admit is now slowly becoming unraveled by the gracious love of God. Now, be aware, sometimes getting back into agreement with God brings some growing pains. The consequences of our actions can hurt, and we must accept them. But once we see clearly the unveiled face of the Lord, our life can become peaceful, meaningful, and productive. We need to focus on the promises that God will be here, God cares, and that God loves each one of us.

Getting back to a focused heart requires us to remember again who God is in our lives after the smoke has blown away and the dust of commotion settles. You may think it strange to say that we can forget who God is, but when forces stronger than our human frames enter in to change the picture on our screen of life, our normalcy is shaken. We must sometimes dig into the corners of our shattered souls and pull God back into our world.

Trouble comes at different times and in various forms for all of us. If our eyes are not centered on Christ, we are no match for the opposition that awaits us. God never gets in the way; He waits until we call out to Him. Then with loving arms, we are spared. For it is written, "Anyone who calls on the name of the Lord will be spared" (Romans 10:13).

Job's story:

The story of a good and righteous man named Job depicts for us how a godly man responds to the intense pressure of tragedy. Job's suffering went beyond what most people could endure. His life was tested physically, mentally, emotionally, and especially spiritually. What was to be revealed through Job's life was that he placed more importance on his relationship with God than on his own well-being. Never did Job blame God for his pain, and his focus did not once waver from God or get misplaced in his tragic, personal experiences.

When we endure times of personal devastation, the book of Job can be our personal manual. Job stared adversity in the face. Let's look specifically at how he managed to keep his hope alive. As we enter this story, we stumble upon a most disturbing conversation in which Satan expressed his belief that Job had found it too easy to follow God, since his life seemed to be perfect, rich with wealth, many children, respect throughout the land, and an adoring wife. But what if these things were tested and threatened? Then, where would the eyes of this good man be focused? As Satan's accusations go on, God forms a reply:

"All right, you may test him," the Lord said to Satan. "Do whatever you want with everything he possesses..." (Job 1:12). That was all Satan needed to hear. He then set off to test him who loved God. It did not take long for the destruction of Job's happiness to begin. First, all his children, wealth and possessions were taken from him. Satan was sure that any human would be crushed by the weight of grief. Instead, Job fell to the ground and cried out in his pain, offering praise to God.

Job said, "The Lord gave me everything I had, and the Lord has taken it away. Praise the name of the Lord." In all of this, Job did not sin by blaming God (Job 1:21-22).

This triggered another assault. Satan replied to the Lord, "Skin for skin – he blesses you only because you bless him. A man will give up everything he has to save his own life. But take away his health, and he will surely curse you to your face" (Job 2:4-5). After this, Job received his second test. He was struck with a terrible case of boils that covered him from his scalp to the soles of his feet. So intense was his pain and irritation that he scratched himself with broken pieces of pottery. Not being able to watch any more suffering, his wife pleaded with him to turn his back on his God.

But still, Job insisted, "You talk like a godless woman. Should we accept only good things from the hand of God and never anything bad?" So in all this, Job still maintained his devotion (Job 2:10).

Next, three of Job's dearest friends came into the picture. However, these friends came not only to offer moral support, but also to attempt to persuade Job. They wanted the torment they saw him suffer to stop and suggested that he must have done something to displease God. Job made countless speeches, replying to every argument they could present. As the trial of Job's integrity and sanity dragged on, he continued to defend his innocence and would not give in to blaming anyone, especially God. This went on for months. How many of us could physically endure the beating our body was suffering and at the same time be relentlessly subjected to the voices of the world snapping in our ears without going mad?

This story benefits us with a moral that is presented through Job's steadfastness and God's wisdom. Job finds himself totally alone and deals with the challenges he faced. Job listened to everything the Lord spoke (Job chapters 38-42), and then he replied, "I know that you can do anything, and no one can stop you. You ask, 'Who is this that questions my wisdom with such ignorance?' It is I. And I was talking about things I did not understand, things too far wonderful for me…. I heard about you before, but now I have seen you with my own eyes. I take back everything I said, and I sit in dust and ashes to show my repentance" (Job 42:2-3 & 5-6).

Job knew that seeing God clearly would bring his life out of the ashes. Focused on the world, we will inevitably get burned, but with God as our Redeemer, that which once was taken is newly restored. The Lord blessed Job in the second half of his life even more than He had in the beginning. He gave Job seven more sons and eight more daughters and more oxen, sheep, donkeys, and camels than he had had before. Job lived 140 years after that and saw four generations of his children and grandchildren. Then he died an old man who had lived a long, good life (Job 42:12-17).

The facts are undeniable; in this world we will be given trouble and, unfortunately, sometimes plenty of it. But take courage as did Job from the knowledge that we have a Redeemer and friend in God. Remain worthy, live with integrity, and hold on to the truth of your salvation, and the hand of the magnificent Creator will be upon you. Wipe away the debris that the accusers of this world throw with these words from scripture, "Stay true to what is right, and God will save you and those who hear you" (1 Timothy 4:16). Our reactions will affect those watching, so be vigilant and choose to praise God anyway!

QUESTIONS TO BEGIN WITH

- Has there been a time you suffered so painfully that you were tempted to walk away from God? What stopped you?

- During our darkest hour, how do we stay convinced that God is there?

- Can you recall a time that you kept your focus totally on God despite what everything else looked like? How did that make a difference in what you experienced?

- What are some of the influences that threaten to take your focus off of God and place it on your situation instead?

- Are there things that we can do to block out worldly distractions? What has been helpful to you?

- Take a moment to write a prayer to God and place your hurting places in His care. Do you believe He is big enough to accomplish that which you have asked?

SCRIPTURES TO CONNECT TO

Job 23:12, Deuteronomy 17:19, Psalm 39:6-7 & 119:28 & 54, 2 Peter 1:20-21

Luke 11:28, Joshua 1:8, Mark 1:17, 2 Corinthians 5:18-21, 1 Peter 2:12

Personal Moments

Personal Moments

Chapter Ten: Back to a Trusting Heart

A Connection to God's Heart – "No eye has seen, no ear has heard, and no mind has imagined what God has prepared for those who love him." -1 Corinthians 2:9

Do we truly trust that God has prepared things for us that we can not even image? We are so busy investing in our security here on earth, but are we prepared for eternity? How do we prepare ourselves for that? I will share an analogy I believe we can all relate to because it is part of daily habit. We invest money month after month into retirement savings, trusting that when we are ready, it will be there. We also make deposits into our spiritual account by living our lives in accordance to God's will. But what happens when, at the end of our lives, we go to make a withdrawal from our spiritual bank, only to find the account empty? The day we were born, God personally opened that account for us. He made the initial investment for us: His love. Over time, that love earned interest called grace, which is free to use at any time. But sadly, some of us do not use it. So, as the last breath of life is taken in, our account closes out. We must make the withdrawal based on our own investment. What is our investment? Loving God back based on the belief that eternal life was given to us by His precious son Jesus. We must not only know this, my friends, we must trust it! As an old hymn goes, heaven asks us to… "Trust and obey for there is no other way to be happy in Jesus, we must trust and obey." Then all that was invested is multiplied unto us beyond imagination. Let me encourage you to choose simply to love God openly. He will speak and reveal all that is necessary for your life to reap a wonderful return if you will trust Him enough to listen.

We should choose to build a foundation of trust. If we build walls, our trust is self-centered, reaching only those inside our inner circle. But if we build those things which the Spirit of God motivates us to, we can potentially touch the world. In quiet moments of reflection, consider this quote shared by a great thinker, Leo Tolstoy: "When I came to believe in Christ's teaching, I ceased desiring what I had wished before. The direction of my life, my desires, became different. What was good and bad changed places." Give these words plenty of time to saturate your thoughts. The point that stands out for me is that only by believing God's Word and seeing Him work in our lives do we learn to trust who He is. Trust is a critical element of faith. A child might believe that her father will catch her, but only when she jumps and lands safely in his arms will she trust him. One leap of faith will soften the way for many more to become possible.

Noah's story:

God said, "Make me a boat…. I am about to cover the earth in a flood…. Noah did everything exactly as God had commanded him" (Genesis 6:5 -22). Noah needed no more instruction to understand and believe what he had to do. Do we fully comprehend the measure of Noah's trust in the One he served? Let's begin by examining exactly where Noah was at this stage of his life. We all can recite the five questions any good detective story covers: Who? Noah. What? Build an ark. Where? In the desert. When? Right away. Why? To spare his family from destruction during the flood.

Noah lived in the desert. Had I lived near him, my first question would have been, why the boat? Of course, reasons didn't matter to Noah; all he had to hear was God's instruction to build it. Can we say the same about our own faith? Do we have to consider the task before we will take action? The pieces of the story we have so far are that Noah was told by God to build an ark in the desert for the purpose of sparing his family from a great flood caused to destroy the human population, and for additional information, the earth has never known rain, yet.

Why does God want to do such a thing? Genesis 6:11 tells us that the whole earth has become corrupt in God's sight. I love revisiting Biblical stories. Nothing has changed in thousands of years! Noah lived at a time when wicked behavior had gotten so out of control that it broke the heart of God, making Him regret ever creating man (Genesis 6:6)! Sound familiar? Have you tuned into the evening news recently? People still rule His world with the wisdom of man, keeping depravity and violence on the throne where God belongs. In contemporary language, a righteous God said, "Game over on account of rain."

Noah's family was spared. God led them each step of the way with every detail down to the last wooden nail. They remained committed to this mission for 100 years! If we think a 500-year-old man making an ark in the middle of the desert did not seem strange enough, the time God required created even further discord with Noah's neighbors. Often we fail to see the sense in our trials when we are in the middle of them. However, Noah saw the sense in following God's instructions, even without an updated weather report!

When does it matter if we have a trusting heart? When can we be sure that it was worth it all? I think that Noah would tell us that it was worth it when he saw those first huge raindrops splattering on the dusty floor of the earth! The next time your faith feels out of place in this world, remember God, trust what He says, and build your ark in obedience to the Lord!

Noah's story did end beautifully and powerfully for him. God confirms His love for those who trust Him through a promise, or in this case, a covenant. A covenant is such a special thing that God only has ever offered three. The first was with Noah, the second with Abraham, and the third was the body and bloodshed of Jesus, connecting all men to God. A covenant life is bound with a connection to God. When the flood was over, God drew a rainbow and placed it in the sky as a sign to us that He is in control and remembers His people. Abraham saw the stars that would number his descendants, and Calvary saw the cross that would save mankind. Have you made your decision to climb onboard the boat that will save you from your proverbial flood, or are you waiting to see what you are building before you begin trusting God, instead of receiving the blessing? The tide may be rising quicker than we think; are you able to tread the elevating water? Salvation is a step away; the blood of Jesus has been given for you. Reach out, He is watching for your return with arms wide open.

QUESTIONS TO BEGIN WITH

- Why do we find it so hard to trust what we cannot see? Do you personally find trust difficult to obtain?

- Do you trust that if God brings us to a trial, He will lead us through it? Why is that the basis of faith?

- Matthew 28:20 says that Jesus can be faithfully trusted to keep every promise, even until the end of the world. Since Jesus can be so trusted, how can that be a help to others as they struggle with faithfulness?

- Think about this passage of Scripture and summarize what it means to you as it pertains to the topic of trusting in God: "This is a true saying: If we die with Him, we will also live with Him. If we endure hardship, we will reign with Him. If we deny Him, He will deny us. If we are unfaithful, He remains faithful, for He cannot deny Himself" (2 Timothy 1:11-13).

- What do you think strengthens our trust in God? Can you use personal examples?

- Like the story of Noah, what are some favorite Scripture verses that build up your trust that God is there during a difficult situation?

SCRIPTURE TO CONNECT TO

Ephesians 5:1-2 & 4:14-15, 2 Corinthians 13:5-6, Genesis 21:1-3, Psalm 145:18

Proverbs 10:3, Daniel 12:3, Hosea 6:13-14, John 6:32-33, Colossians 1:16-17

Personal Moments

Personal Moments

Chapter Eleven: What's New with You?

A Connection to God's Heart – "You don't love me or each other as you did at first! Look how far you have fallen from your first love! Turn back to me again and work as you did at first." -Revelation 2:4-5

Is Jesus calling you as He did once before? It will be an incredible journey back to the heart of God if we hear and heed the whisper to return to Him. Reconnecting to His love requires drawing our attention back to the spiritual world, where everything becomes new in the presence of God. There are moments when we are so far away that something new does not even feel possible. The polarity of God that we felt when we made that initial connection is still pulling us close. If the stories shared throughout this book only convey one message, I hope it is that the path to heaven remains open all the time. The act of being found, having been lost, is the common thread that links us together as we search for our place in this world.

The answer to the question, "What's new with you?" is specific and personal to each of us. Jesus wants us to answer it. In the scripture readings at the chapter's beginning, He asks us to look and see how far we have fallen from His love. That means going back and checking the condition of our hearts so that we are equipped to begin again, renewed, refreshed, and reconnected to the Spirit of God. How do we remember what was before? Well, let's consider three ways to try to experience them for ourselves. An active relationship takes work in order to maintain its vibrancy. To keep passion flowing, both partners must participate, wouldn't you agree? The intimacy of any relationship is dependant not only on the amount of time spent in another's company but also the quality of time spent and what is accomplished during that time together.

The first way to ignite a spark is to turn up the heat! Think of a fire that is dying out. In order to bring back the flames, we need to rekindle the wood. By adding new fuel for the fire, we replace the old, and the fire is brought back. Rekindling all the things that worked in our spiritual relationship is a great technique with which to start our journey toward a strengthened spiritual relationship. Again considering the example of the fire, the wood is necessary for the fire to burn, but if we are not careful to continually replenish its supply, the flame does not last. It is the same with our relationship with God; we must not forget to keep feeding it! Once our emotions are stimulated and our hearts catch fire with the Holy Spirit, we have total access to the awesome new power in our Christian life! Our greatest resource for erupting with spiritual fire is the Holy Words of scripture, for they provide truth and life to those who believe. He has remembered His promise to love and be faithful…. The whole earth has seen the salvation of our God (Psalm 98:3). May these words work as kindling to your spirit, causing the Holy spark from heaven to rain down like a blaze burning wild, spreading to everyone in its path!

The second thing we should do when we walk away is turn around. Revisit Jesus as a new and special friend. Where we left Him is where we will find Him; waiting to be with us. Don't be afraid, He already knows we are coming; nothing is a surprise to the One who knows us so well. The reunion will be worth the trip it took to get there! Revisiting someone we love affords us feelings of comfort, peace, and rest. We are ourselves once again, accepted as a friend of God. How wonderful is the Savior's love for us! It is inconceivable to understand how the same love that has always been available seems so new each time it is accepted! Never be worried about revisiting Jesus, we do not need to hide behind our shame and guilt any longer. Be bold and go back to His extravagant grace. Jesus will always answer the door when He hears us knocking. As our excitement for recovered love feels new, so is God's excitement for the ones who visit Him again, and He rejoices each time we return! Just as in the story of the lost sheep, we are like little sheep, scampering off and not returning home until we find out that things did not go as we well as we thought on our own.

The Story of the Lost Sheep: Luke 15:3-7

It would do us well to reacquaint ourselves with the story that Jesus himself told. It is a tale of His unconditional love for us and his sadness when we stray from Him. From this we know that we can always go home and that we are wanted. He found himself again questioned by the religious leaders of the day about His blatant willingness to eat and drink with the people society labeled as the most despicable. If this man truly was the son of God, how could He surround himself with the likes of such sinners? Jesus' reply came in the form of this illustration.

"If you had one hundred sheep, and one of them strayed away and was lost in the wilderness, wouldn't you leave the ninety-nine others to go and search for the lost one until you found it? And then you would joyfully carry it home on your shoulders. When you arrived, you would call together your friends and neighbors to rejoice with you because your lost sheep was found. In the same way, heaven will be happier over one lost sinner who returns to God than over ninety-nine others who are righteous and haven't strayed away.

Are "ewe" being called home? If so, than go home running. God's arms are opened wide.

The third and final element that we ought to practice is to simply remain on our paths of righteousness. Remain safe in God's love, and there you will find the definition of abiding in Christ. For it is written, "Remain in me, and I will remain in you…. For apart from me you can do nothing…" (John 15: 4-5). Let the new relationship that has been rekindled begin to grow. Eternal life begins when we ask the Spirit to reside in us. We must be cautious and remember that it cost Christ to be with us; therefore, we are required to offer our loyalty to Him in return. This loyalty means that our values and priorities are aligned with God and His standards, not our own. We must evaluate carefully what side we stand on. The world invites God's judgment, but His people are free to accept His love and mercy. Those who remain in that steadfast love will never face rejection from the Father, but will experience contentment of unconditional acceptance based solely on compassion for the tired, hurting, and lost. All this can become new for us once more if we live with a recommitted heart.

Not all of these principles have been news we have not heard before, but we all can take them, share them, and apply them to our lives, because each new day is one which the Lord makes for us! How will you greet the gift of a new day? Will we choose to say, "Good morning, God." Or will we say, "Oh God! It's morning!" In the words of Jesus, we can lighten up and live. Matthew 11:28-30 clearly tells us that we can lay our burdens down at the feet of Jesus. Share in His words, "Come to me, all of you who are weary and carry heavy burdens, and I will give you rest. Take my yoke upon you. Let me teach you, because I am humble and gentle, and you will find rest for your souls. For my yoke fits perfectly, and the burden I give you is light."

Are you ready for the help and love God offers you? Would that be the something new you are looking for? If it is, may you receive your first love and dance forever with the Prince of Peace!

QUESTIONS TO BEGIN WITH

- What has become new in your spiritual journey since beginning this devotional study? What places do you still expect God to take you?

- What is the most significant change you can ask God to make in your life? Will you commit to consistently spending time alone with God so He can speak to you?

- What has been accomplished in your life by spending time with God and connecting with the Holy Spirit?

- Psalm 22:22-23 tells us how we should view the things God has done for us. "Then I will declare the wonder of your name to my brothers and sisters. I will praise you among all your people. Praise the Lord, all you who fear Him! Honor him, all you descendants of Jacob! Show Him reverence, all you descendants of Israel!" This verse lists the things we should be doing. Are they being applied in your life?

- Write a love letter to God, and express your heart to Him.

SCRIPTURES TO CONNECT TO

John 8:10-11, Jeremiah 4:1-2, Psalm 101:1-3, Ephesians 6:13-19, Colossians 4:2

Acts 24-25, Jude 20-21, 1 John 1:9, Ephesians 6:13-18, 1 Timothy 3:16, Luke 12:35-40

Personal Moments

Personal Moments

Afterword

I love observing Christ and His effect on the lives of others. Each life He has touched provides an opportunity to learn more about Him. I am awed by what I have learned from watching those who live their lives with extraordinary faith. In the course of writing this book, more than just words were revealed; God's truths about life and who He is keep my commitment fixed on the correct teaching of His ways. In this work, I celebrate and center on the impact of what a spiritual relationship can have on the world.

Women into Teaching (WIT) is what kept coming to my mind as the pages I have shared with you began to unfold. Whose story are we really wrapped in? It is the love story that God has authored personally with each of us. The body of Christ always serves with the purpose of building people up, never tearing down. WIT is what we need more of, through teaching God's word out of love, but with conviction. I pray that you found the WIT in this book, drawing you closer to a Christ-centered mind.

I do not claim to be a professional theologian. My life is simply captivated by God, and I live in His Word. It's my responsibility that I take seriously. If I can offer any good advice, it would be to fall in love with our Creator; know Him intimately and personally as the one who holds us all together. He has been the example I look to in living out my faith boldly.

None of us are completely able to live out the Christian life without occasionally making a mess of it. The only One who did it right was Jesus, a carpenter from Nazareth. So, look to Him again and go back to the beginning with understanding in His words. Jesus said to the people, "I am the light of the world. If you follow me, you won't be stumbling through the darkness, because you will have the light that leads to life" (John 8:12).

This book is mainly about love – God's love for us, our love for each other, and love for those who have not yet found their way in this world. It has been my prayer throughout the writing process for this devotional that you have experienced Jesus as a friend to us sinners and that we can all live with the attitude that we are free to go and sin no more. My intention was that this study and personal meditation before God would become relevant to all who would embrace the message.

My mother-in-law taught me that the only way to stay in love with the Lord is to actively live it, deeply believe it, and constantly share it. Because my mother-in-law took the time to teach this message to me, I am grateful to be able to share it now with you.

I am excited to announce that our journey into God's Word will continue in the Mother in Love series. Get pumped up! We will be shouting to the Lord as we approach God with authentic hearts filled with worship and thanksgiving! Won't you join me in the fall of 2009, just in time for the holidays, when the third book will be released? Look for the title *Raising the Roof... With Praise and Prayer*. Time in God's word will focus on experiencing power we gain from falling down on our knees. So be prepared to make a joyful, joyful noise!

Until then, be blessed.

About the Author

Nothing qualifies us in writing stories of inspiration better then telling the ones we have lived and seen. This is where Mary's stories come from,Life.

Her struggle with an eating disorder inspired her to reach out in sharing a message of hope to others that recovery is possible through a spiritual journey and faith. That time in her life produced personal growth and physical healing, allowing her to publish a magazine article and first book, How A Mess Became A Message.

Now her focus is on what God can do in a life. She uses the Bible as a daily tool with which she applies the teachings to her life. She has studied the bible in an extensive class for seven years and personal study for fifteen years. All that has offered the knowledgeable background she uses in her writing of daily devotional studies and reflections.

She has been married since age nineteen to the same wonderful man and together they were blessed with a son and two daughters. Their family shares a Christian foundation and a Christ centered life. Mary speaks openly about her struggles and the way God has blessed her life. Currently, she is involved in the Mother in Love conference series which is based on her current and upcoming devotional books.

She and her husband spend time ministering at their church, they mentor a small group of young adults weekly, helping them both personally and spiritually to make the most of the opportunities they have in their life.

They enjoy living close to family and friends in North Wales, Pennsylvania. The family hobbies include camping in their RV, swimming, going to the beach, enjoying people, and all God's creations!

I'm Going Back To…

I'm Going Back To…

I'm Going Back To…

I'm Going Back To...

I'm Going Back To...

I'm Going Back To...